Driving Toward the Moon

Driving Toward The Moon

Poems
by
Barbara Berkenfield

Drawings
by
Susan Berkenfield

SANTA FE

© 2005 by Barbara Berkenfield. All rights reserved.

No part of this book may be reproduced in any form
or by any electronic or mechanical means including
information storage and retrieval systems without
permission in writing from the publisher,
except by a reviewer who may quote
brief passages in a review.

Sunstone books may be purchased for educational,
business, or sales promotional use. For information please
write: Special Markets Department, Sunstone Press,
P.O. Box 2321, Santa Fe, New Mexico 87504-2321.

Library of Congress Cataloging-in-Publication Data:

Berkenfield, Barbara, 1935-
  Driving toward the moon : poems / by Barbara
Berkenfield ; drawings by Susan Berkenfield.
     p. cm.
  ISBN 0-86534-455-8 (pbk.)
  1. Southwestern States—Poetry. I. Title.

PS3602.E7566D75 2005
811'.6—dc22
           2004027008

WWW.SUNSTONEPRESS.COM
SUNSTONE PRESS / POST OFFICE BOX 2321
SANTA FE, NM 87504-2321 /USA / (505) 988-4418
ORDERS ONLY (800) 243-5644 / FAX (505) 988-1025

For
Andy and Jim

Contents

Preface / 11

I. Family and Friends / 17
    Dishes / 19
    Dust / 20
    December News / 21
    Celebration of Karyn / 22
    Mary's Season / 23
    Alice / 24
    Shadows / 25
    Sons Far Away / 26
    The Telegram / 28
    The Seventh Direction / 29
    The Eagle / 30
    Family Photo / 31
    A Chicago Mourning / 32
    Wedding Day / 33
    Joys and Sorrows Recalled / 34
    To Ava, Full of Grace / 36

II. Days, Years, and Seasons / 41
    June Night / 43
    February Thaw / 44
    A May Day / 45
    Summer Memos / 46

August Evening / 47
The New Year / 48
November Morning / 49
Morning Star / 50
Winter Dawn / 51
Gray Dawn / 52

III. Travel / 55

First Safari Day / 57
The Beach / 58
The Visit / 59
Adirondack Evening / 60
Normandy / 61
Spider Woman / 62
Driving Toward the Moon / 64
Maui / 66
A Four Corners Weekend (Red Earth on the Seat of my Pants) / 67

IV. Life In Santa Fe / 71

Sunset Santa Fe / 73
The Docent / 74
Women's Poetry Day / 76
Leaves of Remembrance / 77
The Best of Both Worlds / 78
Corn Dance / 80
Old Men Passing By / 82
The Concert / 84
The Courtyard / 85
Nora / 86

V. The World Around Me / 91
        Sons of Israel / 93
        Syracuse Lament: Pan Am Flight 103 / 94
        April Moon for Ryan / 95
        The Sacred Circle / 96
        Six Months Gone By / 97
        Remembering 9/11 / 98
        In Harm's Way / 99

VI. Coda / 103

        Coda / 105

Preface

My Poetry Brief

I cannot remember a time when I was not writing and, to this day, I recall my childhood delight in the smells and textures of new notebooks, pencils, and erasers. I was very young when I discovered that I could write backwards with ease. I filled notebooks with stories in reverse writing to awe my friends and family with my skill, not at storytelling, but at mirror-image writing. It more than made up for the knuckle raps I received in first grade for writing with my left hand.

I had excellent role models with regard to the importance of creative outlets in my parents and grandmothers. Each had a special escape from routine. My mother played the piano and for years my father took one night a week off from making house calls to enjoy a short story writing course. My maternal grandmother lived with us, and her room was filled with fabric scraps for the quilts she assembled with her foot-pedaled Singer sewing machine. For my paternal grandmother, painting and weaving were not only passions but her professions as an artist and teacher.

Grade school years in the 1940s were filled with grammar, punctuation, and handwriting drills. My generation clogged the air with white dust as we filled wall-length blackboards and broke countless sticks of chalk diagramming sentences. We were prepped through high school that good writing was an essential educational tool regardless of what our future held.

This discipline served me well during my college years, where I am convinced my success as an art history major was largely due to my ability to record a visual experience in clear, well-structured sentences, especially when slides flashed on the screen for less than a minute. I took my first creative writing and poetry courses in college, inspired primarily by our visiting poet-in-residence, Richard Wilbur, on whom we all had crushes.

With marriage and young children, my life allowed little time for writing with the exception of lullabies and rapturous paragraphs in baby books. It was not until we moved to France in 1973 that writing crept back into my life and I began to keep a journal. With our sons now in school, I had more time to write down the thoughts brewing and stewing in my head all day. I then returned later for an objective look at what I had written and began a process of discarding, distilling, and re-writing a poem many times.

I saw my first by-line when I was invited to contribute to the American School of Paris community newspaper, and wrote theatre reviews and travel articles long enough to give me the confidence to submit articles and a few poems for publication after our return to the United States in 1980.

Since moving to Santa Fe I have written feature articles for the magazine supplements published by the *Santa Fe New Mexican* as well as several regional magazines. However, writing poetry has remained a private response to personal and public events ranging from the mundane to the dramatic. If a subject I have been mulling over wakens me in the night, I have learned to get up and write down the words in the dark. If I succumb to sleep instead, they are lost forever.

Some poems germinate for weeks while I am washing, cooking, driving, or marketing, and one day I will finally pull off the road, or stop by the vegetable bins, to take out my small notebook and write the words down so as not to lose them. Even after my follow-up re-writing routine, I may never be truly satisfied and have often re-written a poem when reading it again years later.

The once exception is the poem "Coda" which emerged whole and was never fermented or revised. It is a personal favorite because it has a sense of humor, usually lacking in my work, and addresses a question that has been with me since childhood.

The themes in this small collection of poems written since 1980 come from relationships with friends and family; travel to places of special significance; responses to the physical beauties of my Santa Fe world; observations on a time of year, or a specific time of day; and occasionally my reaction to a specific tragedy.

I thank my sons and husband for their appreciation of my attempts to articulate a depth of feeling through my writing that I can never express verbally.

-Barbara Berkenfield,
Santa Fe, 2004

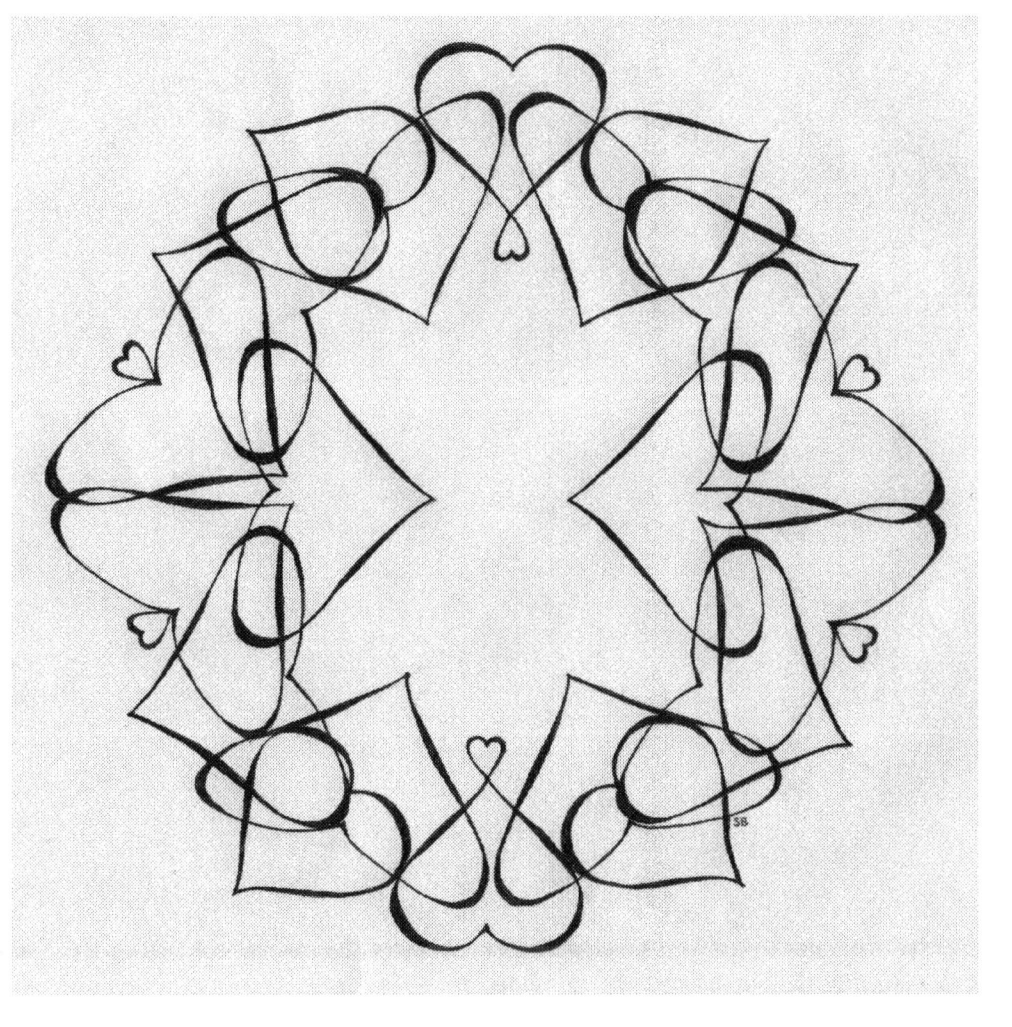

Family and Friends

Dishes

Scrape, rinse, and load
A dishwasher is a one-man operation.
Like TV, it has replaced a time
For family communication.

If they did exist
When I was young
I am very glad
Our home was missing one.

For a teenager learning how to think
The most rewarding conversations
Between my Dad and me
Took place before our kitchen sink.

We were a team several nights a week.
He washed, I dried.
He listened, I would speak.
Full of ideas, ambitions, and energies untapped,
I talked on and on while dishes stacked.

At the dinner table
I never felt as free
To express my many wishes,
As I did when the two of us
Were doing dinner dishes.

January 1983
In memory of my father

Dust

Dusting through our house,
I remember my Pittsburgh childhood.
Mother and grandmother daily
Dusting, sweeping, scrubbing,
To conquer the soot of a coal-hazed city.

Today I regard the film of dust
On family treasures
English tins, Bali masks,
Memories perched on teak and glass,
And jump up to do my duty,

Armed with feather duster
I regard the powdery films
And cobweb lace.
Decide to wait another day
The tedium to face.

January, 1983

December News

The phone rang
On a short, dark December day.
Stunned, I flew away
To wait for results
Of tests and scans
While holding tight
My mother's hands.

Moving through my childhood city
Unheeding Christmas cheer,
I tried to make adult decisions
Controlling the growing fear
Of leaving her behind,
To wait unresisting
The fate of a disease persisting.

December 1983
Pittsburgh

Celebration of Karyn

Celebrations past
Before Christmas fires,
Transient hours of fun
And family sharing.
We held close
To show our caring.

Above a bulky sweater
Your translucent face
Stayed fragile and precious.
You were alone,
Beyond our words and glances,
Experiencing life's edge.

Celebration present
Will be forever.
Your January days are done.
Mature beyond our years
You have escaped our fears.

Now we meet with special touch,
Reach out with love
And bring you back.
You are changed
But still a part of us.

June 23, 1984
For Karyn Angell, celebrating her recovery from leukemia

Mary's Season

Born in autumn,
You were glad
When summer heat had ended.
You wore fall colors
And shades of green,
With jewels of gold,
Jade, and amber sheen.

I think of you happiest in fall,
Gathering multi-colored leaves
And dried flowers
To decorate our hall,
Laughing more at Halloween
Than any other holiday at all.

Today when driving home,
As sunlit reds and yellows
Are dappling the green,
I can miss you,
Child of autumn,
Who for special reasons
Loved this farewell season.

Now back on a hill
Above your country town,
Can you see the brilliant trees above?
Do you feel the blanket
Of the leaves you loved
Like the old gold comforter I craved?

October, 1986
For my mother, who died in January, 1986

Alice

Spring came late this year.
Now rainy days have ended
And today the sun appeared.
Daffodils are gleaming
And willows greening.

Alice left today
Her long, full life now spent.
He went to say goodbye.
And mourn his mother.

For each of us there is no other.
Yet at the last
She knew him still
And thus he is content.

Our last parent is gone.
We are orphans of middle age.
But memories keep them mortal,
And through our sons
The family shall remain.

April, 1987

Shadows

Walking on a winter's night
She comes from behind
To meet my hasting feet
And silent passes by.
Stretching, stopping, shrinking,
She waits to greet me
As I walk home from light to light.

Stepping on shadow trees
Spread across the snow
I recall fierce ceiling beasts
Above my head
On windy childhood nights,
Rushing me to parents' bed.

There I lay between them,
Watching patterns dance above the bed.
From my now snug family berth
I was safe from dragon heads.

December, 1988

Sons Far Away

I: JIM IN KENYA

My setting sun will rise for you.
My rising moon has set for you.
My star-spangled sky will be your dawn.

Sunrise, moonset, star-bright skies
Clock our days,
Your life ahead of mine.

Each sunrise carries my kiss to you.
Each sunset sends my prayers to you.
Each night I choose a star
To beam my love across the ocean
To caress you before waking
On a far continent.

From my southwestern plateau
Of high desert mystique,
I transmit a mother's care to you
Now waking in Maasai land.

Sons Far Away

II: ANDY IN NEW YORK

Our choice made with your blessing,
Our move helped by your caring,
Our fledgling did not leave the nest.
We flew away, leaving you behind
To make your way as you felt best.

Now we hold close through voice and visit.
Briefly you join us in reflected sunset glow
Painting the mountains beyond our plateau.
Together we travel the moonlit patterns
Of our desert space.

Here, then gone.
We are separated once again.
Supported by your love and sharing,
I find the words to express
How much we miss you
In Jim's Kenya letter:
"Further away, closer in the heart.
Stronger the love the longer apart."

December, 1989, following our move to Santa Fe

The Telegram

The birth announcement
Came by telegram.
This treasured souvenir
Has been aging
On the desk for thirty years.

Today's phone call
Announces his death.
Shot in a city phone booth
For a wallet he didn't have
By a random creature
Uncaring of our loved one.

As the darkness swells
For a summer storm,
My anger grows
Like the anvil-shaped cloud
Spreading above our mountains.

Unlike the storm
Which will release its rage
In hail and rain,
My anger will find no ease
And I cannot erase "if only..."

A newspaper clipping
Is folded with the telegram
In its faded envelope.
Which now rests in a drawer,
A souvenir of a godson
Who lives no more.

July 30, 1990, in memory of godson John Reisenbach, killed in New York City

The Seventh Direction

A cycle is completed.
Time now to consider
The next direction
You are taking.

Go round the circle
To seek wisdom from the guardians.
As you learn what they can teach.
Remember to leave a gift
When you encounter each.

Eagle soars above with Father Sky.
Mole waits below in Mother Earth.
Mountain Lion crouches in the North.
Bear stands bravely to the West.
South sits the Badger,
And Wolf paces in the East.

When you have done
Then you will follow only one,
The seventh direction,
Which is of your own making.

*May, 1991: Jim's graduation from Cornell.
According to American Indian sculptor
Doug Coffin, the seventh direction
is the direction you are taking.*

The Eagle

When the time comes
To leave my loves
And fly alone,
It is my dream
To be forever free
Above my mountain home.

I will be suspended
On milky mists
Among majestic peaks
In the pure, wild air
Beyond the world of care.

Here as I glide
I will hold close
To life's memories
Held within my wings.

Husband and children
Will know where to find me
As I sail high
Forever free
In the ethereal sky.

*June, 1992. Inspired by a painting
by Dale TerBush*

Family Photo

A fading photograph of my family
Posed in the Luxembourg Gardens
Was melting behind the glass.
We were fast fading,
Dissolving in the Santa Fe sun.

Barely visible in our 1970s clothes,
We sat with arms around each other
In bell-bottom jeans
And coats of leather,
Facing the camera together.

Old negatives are discovered,
And we are restored,
A happy couple with two young sons,
Smiling at our friend
On a Paris winter day,
A world and a lifetime away.

*Christmas, 1994, inspired by a family photo
dated February 1976*

A Chicago Mourning

Closely bound since college years
Despite distances of grown-up lives,
You are all together once again
To say goodbye to cherished friend.

Stunned that he is gone,
Saddened that your love and caring
Could not keep him with you,
Your youth has ended here.

You could not mend his inner pain
Or convince him to stay with you
Through the years ahead.
His struggle wore him out,
And he made a choice.

You must only hope
He has found the peace
He was so desperately seeking.
Respect his decision to search beyond.

Be thankful for his friendship.
He did not leave you easily.
Mourn your loss, and know
His memory is forever in your keeping.

February 1999: In memory of Jim Peters

Wedding Day

Our life's journeys
And never ending trails
Bring each of us here today
To become part of the circle
Of your happiness.
Our colors and varieties intertwine
Like the wildflowers of this wreath
Closely tied to last forever.

Like the spiral mazes
Pecked on walls of ancient caves
We will live on
In your memories,
Our threads passing down
Through the generations.

And your wedding day
In this land of high desert
Mountain and mesa,
Will be remembered always
In these hearts around you.

May the platinum moon and golden sun
Shine on you
And keep you close.
May the earth, stars and planets
Embrace you,
Just as we embrace you
In this circle of family love
Never to be broken.

October 2, 1999
For Jim and Sue on their Wedding Day,
Santa Fe, New Mexico

Joys and Sorrows Recalled

Bundled in winter coats,
They stood small in the cold
Florescent glare of station lights,
Waiting for me in the late hours
Of the snowy winter night.
On my first train trip home.

Too soon it seemed
We hugged with goodbye tears.
I left them behind,
My thoughts racing ahead
To the challenges, work, and play
Of a college life far away.

This was the beginning
Of the joys and sorrows
Of reunion and departure.
The years of a thousand goodbyes
Ended with those final trips,
When no one came to meet me.

Meanwhile we were lovers
Kissing on train platforms
Until we were joined forever.
Soon our own children
Were running to meet us
From college and worlds beyond
With their special love,
And leaving us too soon
Within the sadness of separation.

Each airport and station
Is the stage for a moment in the life
Of each person passing through.
Parents and children,
Lovers, friends, and siblings
Meet and part.
Lone men and women hug their phones.
There is a story in every embrace,
Every held hand, laugh,
Tear, and even stony silence.

January, 2004

To Ava, Full of Grace

Your bright angled face
And long-legged stride
Retained a youthful grace
And special beauty,
A rose still in full bloom.

Wife for nearly sixty years,
Mother of your own
Four accomplished graces,
With us yesterday,
Today you're gone.

Arthritic handicap ignored,
You stepped ahead
With energy and joy
Through eight decades
Of leadership and love.

Ava aviatrix,
A female pioneer.
Member of a daring few
Who made history
Flying across our country.

Walking with purpose,
No hint that you were leaving
Could we detect.
Can it really be that
You are gone?

Your presence cannot be replaced
Ava, full of grace.
You strode across the line,
Leaving us behind
To mourn our loss.

Yet I am happy you escaped
Age's heartbreaking gifts
Of suffering and pain.
Your strength of spirit
Will nourish us who still remain.

August 10, 2004: In memory of Ava Carmichael

Days, Years, and Seasons

June Night

Barely touching on a breathless summer night
 I recall an airless room in an old camp dorm
Where we lay in the same moist cocoon
Twenty years ago.

The traffic roar of our Vespa ride
Was still humming in my ears
As I lay by your side.
I was sure if we stayed close
No harm would come to us.

Then I waved good-bye,
Unsure of your promises
As you sailed to meet
The year of your dreams.

You returned to me
And through all our years together
We still lie,
On breathless summer nights,
Barely touching.

June 1980

February Thaw

Running our morning mile,
Dog and I leash-linked
Beneath a winter sky.
Crust on stale snow
Breaks brittle underneath
Our steady beat.

Trees creaking,
Branches squeaking,
Chattering birds and squirrels
The only life in a landscape
Black, gray, and white.

Later by the sudden change
Of sun and breeze,
Uniquely strange,
Our world melts
In a watercolor wash
Of browns and greens.

Uncurl the laurel.
Unfurl the leaves.
Pools of water splash our lawns
Reflecting promise of spring to come.

February, 1982
Published in The Tower *magazine*
of The Masters School in February, 1988

A May Day

As rains abate
Dogwood and cherry blossoms
Open with a sigh.
Magnolia petals fall to the ground,
While bird calls pierce
The fresh-scrubbed sky.

Perennials inch upward,
Stretching in discovered sun
And the dog lies
On a bed of clover,
Dreaming of a run.

Forsythia blossoms
Dulled by the rain,
Now lie defeated on the green.
A gutter trickling the only sound,
And dandelion heads abound.

Our world is new again.

May 1983
Published in The Tower *magazine*
of The Masters School in June, 1989

Summer Memos

Vacation:

Sun shatters lake light
That reflects the crystal sky

A sigh slides from my heart.
I ease into nothingness
And forget my part.

Daydream:

I see only a bright sail.
I hear only my heartbeat.
I feel only the sun.
I taste only the wine
As I touch the sky.

The Island:

Treeless it reclines,
A dinosaur bathing.
Gulls sit along its spine,
A line of armor plates
Silhouetted against the evening sky.

July, 1983
Lake George

August Evening

Dinner's done.
The boys have gone
To summer fun.
We stay on
Sipping wine,
Too hot to move inside.

As darkness comes
Fireflies flicker
In garden shadows.
Katydids' stridulating songs
Inspire us to remember
Our own past summer nights.

Young, undrained by work
And August heat,
We loved that
After-dinner time of day
When the screen-door slammed
As we ran out to play.

August, 1983
Hartsdale house

The New Year

Each year we meet
To celebrate the ending,
Beginning of the new.
How strange it seems
In winter's chill
To consecrate renewal
With the world so dark and still.

Warmed more by friendship
Wine and fire,
Than by a day of fragile sun,
We share our past years
Joys and sorrows,
With old songs re-sung.

Yet time is not frozen
Like the pond outside.
Our talk clicks forward
To dreams ahead,
And we continue living
As the world rewinds.

January, 1984
Published in Holiday Musings
by American Arts Association, p. 75

November Morning

Color muted by the hoar,
A hint of blue and rose
Above the morning mist
Threads through tenacious trees,
With branches bare
But not yet brittle.

Dog and I cross sugar-coated leaves,
And frost-powdered grass,
Their crunch the only sound
As we rejoice in the soft silence
On this still November morn.

November, 1984

Morning Star

Here he comes
The morning star
Gliding up my window
Before the dawn.

He leads the way
Each winter's day
With an invisible thread
Pulling up the sun
From below my horizon
Of silhouetted desert trees.

Across the way
The new moon rests
On crescent back
Against a bank of clouds,
Facing the morning star.

As they rise together
The star stays bright.
The moon turns pale
While the cloud bank lightens,
Stretches, spreads to tatters,
And dissolves into the sunrise.

January, 1990

Winter Dawn

Facing the night
A subtle change of light
Has stopped my dreams.

Stars are quickly fading,
Except the morning star
Shines brighter as it rises
Above the ristra-strung portal.

The salmon tint
Spreading on the horizon
Recalls my mother's
Velvet powder puff.

Pink and blues fade
Into a cold white light
As thin arrow streaks of cloud
Reflect the rose of coming dawn.

February, 1990

Gray Dawn

First light reveals
A monoprint of heavy clouds.
Mountains are in hiding.
The black tree line forms
A lacy silhouette.

The world is shades of gray
Like my hair
In morning's mirror.
Am I already
At the other end of the rainbow?

But here in Santa Fe
Clouds only last a day.
Tomorrow the sun will shine,
Color will return,
And I will be young again.

March, 1990

Travel

First Safari Day

The sturdy, aging van
Bounces along a road of dust.
Tall, elegant Maasai
Swathed in beads
And clay-red robes
Wave and stare as we pass by.

Friends and family
View the vast treeless plain
Through camera "eyes."
Unincumbered, I scan the horizon
And am the first to shout
"Elephant at ten o'clock."

Our first safari day
Ends at dinner in the lodge
Where we talk in awe
Of gazelle and buffalo herds,
A pride of lions in the grasses,
The unexpected variety of birds.

When darkness falls
And stars and silence fill the sky
The beasts watering below
Move up into the yard,
And we fall asleep to the sound
Of zebras grazing by our door.

April, 1976, Kenya

The Beach

As my feet slap softly on the wet sand,
My family rides the waves
Oblivious to my fears
Of the surf breaking harshly at my side.

Yet I love the beach's beauty,
The smell and drama of the sea.
And I search for a gift this one may offer,
While I recall past treasures dear to me.

Danish amber, Mombasa starfish,
Beach glass of the Cote d'Azur,
Cap Ferret's fragile scallops,
The chalk covered flinty rocks of Etretat,
And tiny shells of now peaceful Omaha.

We have walked the shores of oceans, lakes, and seas,
Explored the beaches of Europe, Africa and our homeland.
I think of the many colors of their sands,
The shapes of their stones and shells,
And my family's voices fade within the surf's roar
As I walk on.

August 1980, Long Island

The Visit

Shivering in the unfamiliar room
I watch a pale, cold light
Expand to reveal ghostly forms
Crouching on the floor.
I stare uneasily at the back-packs
Waiting for our journey to begin.

Yesterday we stood at the canyon's rim,
Silently watching cloud shadows undulate
Across timeless layers of plateau.
We searched for the river,
A miniature green line a mile below,
Eons back in time.

The door opens and sons appear
In the Canyon hikers' attire
Of faded jeans and flannel shirts.
Excited voices of preparation
Surround me as I walk to clothes
Waiting patiently on the chair.

It is time to go.

March 1983
The Grand Canyon

Adirondack Evening

Fir-blanketed mountains
Lie back through
Shades of green
To distant gray.

Slate sky
Reflects silver
In the lake,
Like mercury on water.

White-tipped waves
Come in to lick
And slap the boats
Lying on the shore.

Sister of the widow
On her walk
Looking out to sea,
I wait for my fishermen
Coming home to me.

September, 1983

Normandy

Standing at attention
In rows to the horizon,
We are white sentinels
Of cross and star,
Casting shadows on manicured lawns,
Guarding your sons and fathers.

High on our windswept cliff,
Above the tranquil beach,
We patiently await our visitors.
There is no cause for hurry,
We are nine thousand strong.
We will remain forever.

June 6, 1984
Omaha Beach, Normandy, France

Spider Woman

Farewell my family
In our peaceful valley
Sheltered by strong red canyon walls.

I must leave my web
Between my sister-brother spires
To rise above the soaring birds
Before the spreading anvil clouds
Herald the evening storm.

The foreign warriors,
Who brought pain and death
To our sheltered canyon caves,
Have also brought a blessing.

Remember time past
When I taught you to weave
The cotton grown on canyon soil.
Now these Spanish warriors
Have brought a sheep
With fleece of finest wool.

I go to teach the cousins
Of our Diné Nation
To card, spin, and weave
This blessing into blankets
To be cherished by all
Who live above our valley.

When I leave that upper land,
Where mountains move
Like the sea beneath cloud shadows
And turn blood red at summer sunsets,
I will come back to help you
Spin and weave this wondrous wool.

Be patient and wait for me.
We will again be one
Within the golden stillness
Of our deep canyon home,
Where the sun, moon, and stars
Protect us from the world above.

July, 1991: Canyon de Chelly, Arizona

Driving Toward the Moon

Day One:

Christmas memories are fading
As our children vanish in the morning fog.
We look back through a mist of tears
And wave goodbye.

The San Joaquin valley sun
Warms our backs
While we picnic in a flat world
Of cultivated fields.

The velvet hills of the Sierra Nevada
Wrinkle like a Shar-Pei's coat
In the hazy winter light,
And windmills wave farewell
As we descend into the desert.

Day Two:

Fighter planes cavort above us
When we cross the Mohave scrub
And climb through gentle hills
To a barren desert world
Framed by jagged ridges.

A ghostly disk appears
In the pale late-day sky
And we are in a different world.
In our own lunar landscape
We are driving toward the moon.

Our day ends
In a crisp winter Flagstaff night
Where food, bed, and books
Welcome us back to earth.

Day Three:

A cloudless mountain morning
Follows us across a high treeless plateau.
We descend the mesa's eastern slope
Into gray Gallup's vacant Sunday streets.

The beauty of Red Rock Canyon
Beckons us eastward
As we drive within the boundaries
Set by eighteen wheelers.

We are home
Surrounded by bags, gifts, food, and mail.
Our dog stretches in relief.
We walk through familiar rooms
And celebrate a safe and happy
Ending to the year.

By driving toward the moon
We have found the road home.

January, 1999: after Christmas
with Andy, Suzie, Jack and Colette

Maui

Tiny shell and coral shards
Are the only hints of secrets
Beyond the pristine beach,
As I submerge to rocky reefs below.

Sharp lava rocks
Harsh and lifeless up above,
Now wave in filtered sunlight
And frame a wondrous garden glow.

Oh, to be a mermaid for a time,
To understand the clicking sounds
Of growing coral
And learn the patterns of this world
Before returning to the one I know.

December 1984, Maui

A Four Corners Weekend
(Red Earth on the Seat of my Pants)

The outline of red earth
On the seat of my pants
Remains a souvenir
Of our Saturday San Juan River run.

My old white canvas Keds
Have dried to a pale shade of red,
Stained by soft river mud.
They look sort of cool.

The bottom of my tan shorts
Has turned burnt sienna
From my Sunday lunch seat
On the Twin Rocks Trading Post terrace.

My socks unfold in a mist
Of powdery talc
While the dog shakes herself
And disappears in a red cloud.

Weekend memories are captured
On a canvas of earth tones
Brought home from an ancient world
Of dust, mud, and mesa.

Memorial Day Weekend, Bluff, Utah 2003

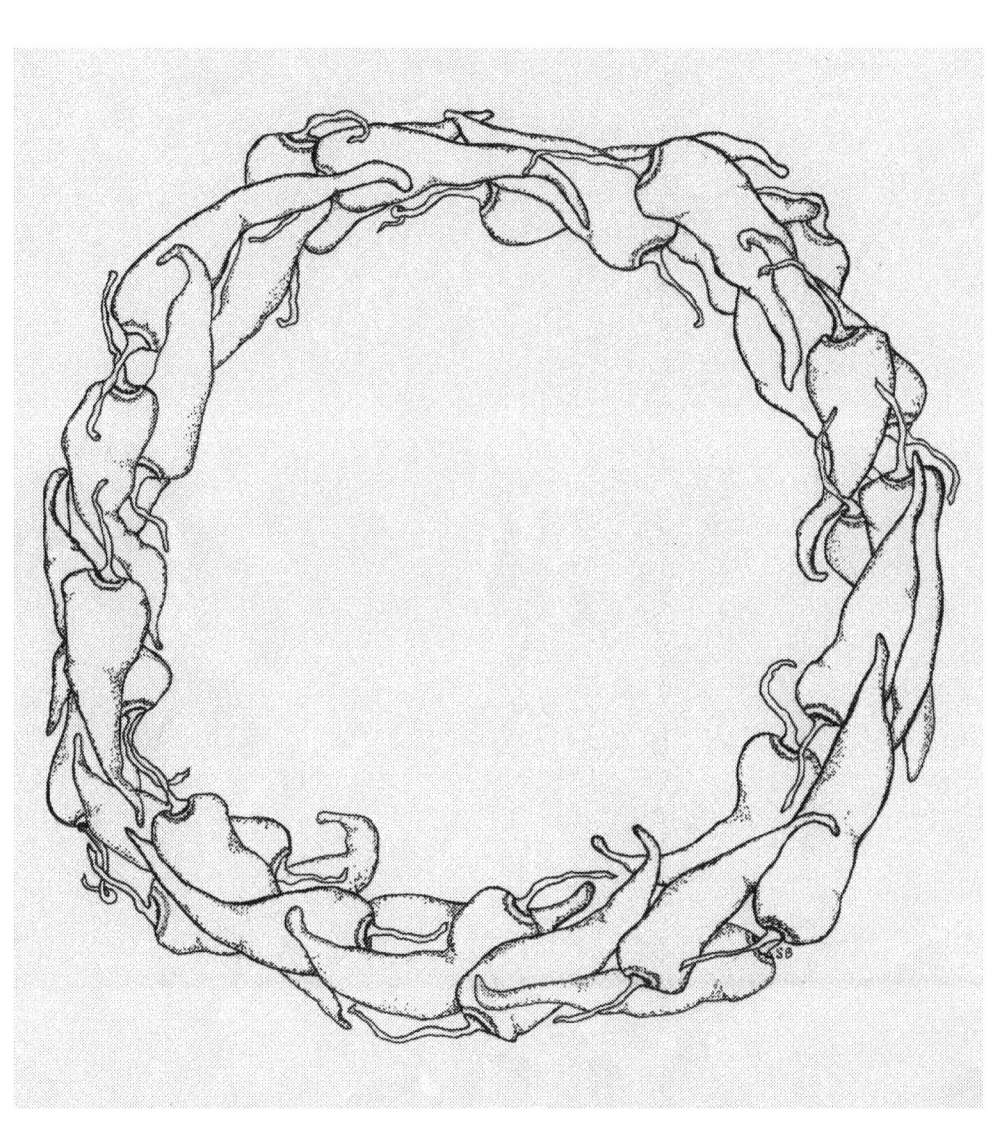

Life In Santa Fe

Sunset Santa Fe

Today's sunset pales opposite
The beauty of its reflection
On the Sangre de Cristo range.
The mountains are crowned by
Evening's roseate clouds
Moving slowly southward.

Our own pinon and juniper
Are tipped with gold
As the sky's purples, pinks
And shades of blue and gray
Merge to create the perfect end
To a classic Santa Fe day.

My camera has no film.
My mind must snap this scene
To hold for life's end,
So that I may say farewell
Inside the memory
Of this special sight.

January, 1990

The Docent

Driving toward town
From my high desert home,
I revere the mountains
Clothed in summer velvet,
And salute the roadside blooms,
Wildflowers weekly changing.

Joining city traffic
I am swallowed by trucks
Waving diesel plumes of progress.
Ignoring motel and fast-food funnel,
I focus ahead to the Ortiz peaks
Standing sharp and crisp
Against the hazy Sandia range.

Shoulders tense from
The rush of morning chores,
Thoughts still churning with
Errands yet undone,
I turn down the country road
Past horses prancing
At their morning rounds.

Slowing down on slippery gravel
I unwind as I approach
The red clay road
Packed hard from last night's rain.
Its smooth surface shines like pottery,
Leading me to Las Golondrinas.

Walking through the tranquil dust
I absorb the peace from old adobe.
Cares and worries disappear
As I change to clothing
Of Spanish Colonial Days.
I am ready to speak of life and hardships
Of another time.

*August, 1990. Published in the January 1991
edition of* El Paraje, *newsletter of*
El Rancho de as Golondrinas

Women's Poetry Day

The mayor of Santa Fe
Has declared this Women's Poetry Day.
I settle on a banco
At Burnt Horses bookstore
To listen and compare,
Find inspiration or despair.

New arrival in this town
I recognize no face.
Only friends and family far away
Have heard my secret voice
And I am happy with this choice.

Four young women read
With energy, warmth,
Love, and concern
For their Santa Fe world
Under the shadow of Los Alamos.

I feel brittle, drier than the rest.
My voice more timid
Even at its best.
Yet driving home with country songs,
I discover my voice is weak,
But not yet gone.

March 17, 1990

Leaves of Remembrance

Snow trims the Sangre peaks.
Frost rims the aspen trees.
Chamisa's bloom now olive drab.
In our high mesa land
A lone cottonwood flares yellow
As I pass its sheltering wash.
While town trees compete for attention
In our Southwest autumn.

Ristras, apples, dried flowers and
Piles of pumpkins herald Halloween.
Skeletons announce Day of the Dead.
This veneration of our ancestors,
Gives a continuity to life
From one world to the next.
Just as autumn's changes
Prepare us for a winter rest.

I unwrap a package,
Holding pressed New England leaves.
Yellows, reds, and browns
Of maple, beech, and oak.
A son's note explains
His wish to send a gift
Of fall treasures from the East.

No gift more thoughtful,
Or sent with greater love,
Reviving family memories
Of the brilliant autumns
Shared with growing sons.
I arrange them with care,
In a sweet sadness for a life now past.

October, 1990

The Best of Both Worlds

Above our sheltered home
A storm of blue-black clouds,
Hurling angry lightning
Against the fiery sunset glow,
Is caught in a photo
To remain forever in my sight.
Its rage is forgiven
For the gift of snow and rain
It brings to succor the coming spring.

Below we are safely anchored
Within old adobe walls.
Fashioned by time and use,
Rebuilt by family hands,
They hold their sacred memories
And preserve the beauty
Of our ancient earth.

Now the warmth of hearth
And golden candle light
Reflect outside upon the snow
And welcome you to share
The blessings of man and nature.
The best of both worlds
Offered on this stormy night.

December, 1991

"...the Moors use the term *baraka* to describe a special character in places or things. Many centuries ago, the word alluded to a quality imparted abruptly and dramatically – lightning bolts were among its most powerful causes... Gradually, it came to be regarded as a trait...that accumulates very slowly, culminating eventually

in a sort of spirituality that has been described as *blessedness*. ...adobe provides a natural habitat for the deep-rooted memory known as *baraka*... Adobe bricks made on long-used ground will be...a synthesis of the present with the shards, ashes, and other traces left by life in the past."
Brewer & McDowell, *The Persistence of Memory*, Museum of New Mexico Press, 1990. pp. 20-21.

Corn Dance

Standing on the hard packed earth
In the hot white morning light
We await the drum.
The drum is coming,
The deep beat thrumming,
Men's voices deeply humming.

Led by an elder,
Whose strong, steady stroke
Enters my heart
And becomes its beat,
The drum group stops before us.
Young and old men's
Voices chant the traditions.

Now pass by in thickening dust
The corn-husk-headed koshari
Dancing, urging, encouraging
The rows of dancers to follow
With their sound of rattles and shells,
Amid the sweet scent of pinon boughs.

Snaking slowly down the plaza,
Men's moccasins firmly keep the beat.
Women step delicately on bare feet.
Elders monitor each row,
Blessing with the cornmeal,
Adjusting sashes, skirts and bells.

Rattles shaking, hair feathers waving,
Foxtails swinging, bells on leg bands ringing,
The men and boys'
Painted bodies warp the pattern.

Tablitas crowning long glossy hair
Knotted sashes swaying,
Pine boughs waving,
The women and girls'
Black dresses weft the pattern.

The procession binds us tight
In harmony with earth and sky and light.

*August, 1995, Santo Domingo Pueblo,
New Mexico*

Old Men Passing By

I

His coat flaps and billows
Around his fragile frame
Bowed into the wind.
So neatly dressed
With moustache trim,
He moves with purpose
Toward the bus stop.
I wait at the light
And watch his painful gait.
Was he always so small and spare,
Or has he shrunk with age?
Will the bus take him to a loving wife,
A warm adobe home
Where dog and supper wait?
Or only to a lonely room
Where he will sit by a heater
In the evening gloom?

II

He stands by the cemetery fence,
Leathery walnut skin,
Unshaven and dull-eyed.
Dark and dusty,
Clothing rusty,
He waits so patiently.
Is it for a friend or son
Who will take him home
To a chair on the portal
To watch the sunset?
Or will he sleep alone
Beneath the stars,
Wrapped in a blanket,
Remembered by none?

III

Hand out, thumb up,
A white-whiskered scarecrow
Walks backward up the road.
He wends this way
Each end of day.
As I pass him by
I wonder who will meet him.
Has he been missed today
By grandchildren out at play?
Earlier I have seen him
Sitting on the plaza in the sun.
Is this his daily goal?
Or is there work he seeks
And then retreats?

IV

These old men
Are part of my day's end.
If they are not in sight
I wonder if they have faded
Into shadows with the end of light.
Has their fragile strength
To walk home in the night
Been broken by their lonely life?

December, 1995

The Concert

The Ga'an Dancer poses
Above the quartet.
His arms stretch wide
Hands holding wands
As if he were conducting.

A drum group frozen in bronze
Sits on a table
Chanting to the music.
All are listening.

Painted birds and deer
On ancient pots,
Carved stone couples
Standing for eternity,
All are listening.

Navajo rugs sway
And beaded sashes flow
Down the walls
As Haydn fills the room.
All are listening.

We share this welcome space
With all the arts,
Bound together by the melody
As we all are listening.

*May 25, 1997: a chamber music concert
at a friend's home*

The Courtyard

Beneath a pale evening sky
Pink and white blossoms,
Suspended from sharp black branches,
Tremble in the April breeze
Against the weather-streaked adobe wall.

April, 2000, Canyon Road

Nora

The animated gestures
Of Mud Woman's small, smooth hands
Accentuate her passion
As she speaks to us
Of her people
Working with the clay
For centuries.

Gathering, cleaning,
Mixing ash and kneading
Are acts which form
A center for the lives
Of each generation.

Clay is the anchor of her life
And becomes the outlet
For her talents.

She has taken tradition
Into her heart,
And from it creates
Clay figures of whimsy and wisdom
To express her thoughts
About her contemporary world.

Multi-media Mud Woman
Explores, studies, and analyzes
Through writing, lecturing,
And film-making
But always through the clay.

We are in awe of her life,
So centered and calm,
With every moment full of creativity
And positive energy.

When I work in garden dirt
My hands become dry and cracked.
Her hands, immersed in clay
Every day of her life,
Become more beautiful
As the clay nourishes her being.

*July, 2003, following a lecture by
ceramic artist Nora Naranjo Morse*

The World Around Me

Sons of Israel

A day of brilliant sunshine
As autumn bursts of color
Blossom on the trees.

While color spreads
So does the news
And the vivid splashes
Are like massacre blood
Staining our world.

Sons of Israel
Children of the Holocaust
May even you have proven
To err can be inhuman.
Hatred to this extent
Cannot be what history has meant.

As we rake leaves in dull-hued piles
I think of bodies stacked against a wall
Six hundred is not six million
Yet if you could condone this event
What hope for man is left?

October 1982

Syracuse Lament
Pan Am Flight 103

Sons and daughters,
Sisters, brothers,
Fathers, mothers,
Infants,
Lovers.

Our children
Received in Scotland
Without warning
By families unsuspecting.

The bagpipes play
"Lament for the Children"
As we now mourn together.
No comfort that our loves
Were the chosen ones
For a selfish act of man.

The Talmud story tells us
The Lord gave us diamonds
And may take them any day
But terrorists, not the Lord
Have taken ours away.

How can we be assured
Our precious diamonds,
Denied their futures
In this world,
Are with the Lord?

We must share this grief together.
Forever.
Amen.

January, 1989
Published in Poetic Voices of America,
Summer Edition, 1990 by Sparrowgrass

April Moon for Ryan

The room is day-bright.
The ground glows white.
The trees stand black
On round shadow puddles
As the moon rides high.

I think of Ryan
Now at rest from his war
With suffering and shame.
The country which once shunned him
Now mourns and praises his name.

His youth ravaged by man's mistake,
He sought to slay the dragon.
Facing taunts and pain with manner brave,
Our warrior son lost the battle
But won our hearts forever.

On this full moon night
May Ryan be at peace.
May we remember always
The gift of his example,
And treat with love
The many other lives to save.

*April 11, 1990, teenager Ryan White
died of AIDS following a long and public
struggle to go to high school while he was ill.
He contracted AIDS from a blood transfusion
several years earlier.*

The Sacred Circle

East above our mountains
The full moon rises
Behind a misty veil.
Above the jewel-lit city
It shimmers,
A circle of liquid silver.

Ring around the rosy,
Dance around the maypole,
Tops, hoops, and yo-yos,
A wedding band,
The sacred sipapu,
The man in the maze,
The black holes of the universe,
Our earth and planets,
All these circles are
Symbols of oneness and mystery,
Balance and harmony.

Yet the circle
May become
A symbol of destruction
As holes in the ozone
Expand above us.

March, 1992

Six Months Gone By

Ribbons red white and blue
Still tremble gallantly
As they slowly fade
On our schoolyard fences.

They gently blow away.
Fences are no longer covered
As ribbons disappear into the air
And all grows quiet here.

War continues far away.
Sporadic terrorist alerts
Keep us from complacency
As the tower images dissolve.

Fearful bearded faces grow dim
And we wonder if we will forget our losses.
But while one shredded ribbon remains
Our lives will never be the same.

March, 2002

Remembering 9/11

Each day as I pass the schoolyard fence
The flutter of fading ribbons,
Tied there by our children,
Waves to me
And I remember.

Now only a sun-bleached few
Of red, white, and blue
Tenaciously remain,
Clinging to the wire mesh,
Determined that we will not forget.

September 11, 2002

In Harm's Way

The photo of a young soldier,
Sitting with his comrades against a tank
On the desert floor,
Spotlights the rifle in his lap.

The caption says he is cleaning his gun.

But he is looking to the horizon,
His expression blank with fatigue,
Not thinking of his gun,
Perhaps dreaming of home.

Is he wondering why he is there?

Iraqis are fighting back.
Why such surprise?
Would we just say welcome,
Or use any trick to defeat our invader?

Can we look at the destruction
And not hurt in our hearts?
A world and religion we little understand
Does not mean we cannot be moved.

April, 2003

Coda

Coda

When I come back
A bird in flight,
A sleek wild cat,
A silent stone
Or haggard crone
Of flesh and bone,
Will house or shell
Be my next home?

When I come back
All dressed in white,
A blue ribbon pulling
Hair back tight,
Or dull and starving
In the dust,
Will the world around me
Turn to rust?

When I come back
As king or queen,
A tiny mouse
Or insect green,
Will I remember
What I've seen?

It is wondrous to imagine
Who I might be
In the year 5003.
Yet if I come back
As man or tree
Nothing can improve
On being me.

December, 1984

www.ingramcontent.com/pod-product-compliance
Lightning Source LLC
Chambersburg PA
CBHW072200100426

42738CB00011BA/2489